# LIFE LESSONS
# I LEARNED

# FROM MY DOG

Illustrated by Emma Block

First published in Great Britain in 2019 by LOM ART, an imprint of
Michael O'Mara Books Limited
9 Lion Yard
Tremadoc Road
London SW4 7NQ

A CIP catalogue record for this book is available
from the British Library.

Papers used by Michael O'Mara Books Limited are natural,
recyclable products made from wood grown in sustainable
forests. The manufacturing processes conform to the
environmental regulations of the country of origin.

ISBN: 978-1-912785-08-7 in hardback print format
ISBN: 978-1-912785-09-4 in ebook format

3 5 7 9 10 8 6 4

Designed and typeset by Claire Cater

Printed and bound in China

Follow us on Twitter @OMaraBooks

www.mombooks.com

THIS BOOK IS DEDICATED TO MY FATHER,
PAUL BLOCK, AND OUR DOG, SAMMY (2003–2019)

I've always grown up around dogs. My parents' first dog, Max, was just a few months old when I was born and we used to chew books together on the living room floor when we were both teething. Later in life my parents got another dog, Sammy, who was the beloved family dog for fifteen years.

As an adult, visiting my parents always means an excited furry friend meeting me in the hallway, long walks on the beach on a Sunday afternoon, evenings spent curled up on the sofa together and an abundance of dog hair on everything. I have always loved dogs and always will. They are eternal optimists, silly, playful, forgiving and endlessly loyal, which is why we can all learn a little something from them.

Emma Block

ALWAYS BE ENTHUSIASTIC

OVERCOME FEAR WITH LOVE

DON'T HOLD GRUDGES

PLAY EVERY DAY

# ACCEPT

# YOURSELF

# SHOW COMPASSION

SHOW YOUR LOVED ONES
HOW MUCH YOU CARE

ENJOY THE JOURNEY

LOVE UNCONDITIONALLY

# JUMP FOR JOY WHEN YOU'RE HAPPY

# GREET THE ONES YOU LOVE

YOU ARE NEVER TOO OLD TO PLAY

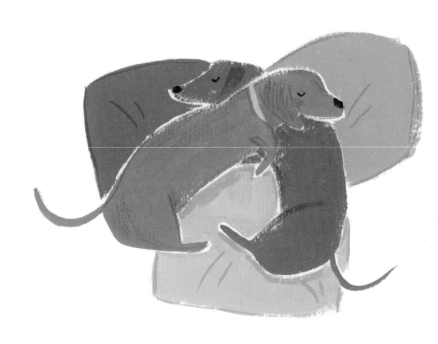

APPRECIATE ONE ANOTHER

FORGIVE EASILY

# TAKE LIFE AT YOUR OWN PACE

# SAVOUR YOUR FOOD

BE LOYAL

ENJOY THE SILENCE

LIVE IN THE MOMENT

# STAY

# FOCUSED

FRIENDSHIP CAN BE EASY

DRINK LOTS OF WATER

# DO THE THINGS THAT MAKE YOU HAPPY

ANY JOB IS WORTH DOING WELL

# STAY ACTIVE

TREAT YOURSELF

GO AFTER THE THINGS THAT
ARE IMPORTANT TO YOU

ALWAYS

MAKE EYE

CONTACT

MOVE PAST YOUR MISTAKES

SPEND LOTS OF TIME OUTSIDE

# DON'T BE AFRAID TO GET MESSY

ENJOY THE QUIET MOMENTS

ENJOY

THE

VIEW

TRUST YOUR INSTINCTS

DIG FOR BURIED TREASURE

NEVER PRETEND TO BE
SOMETHING YOU'RE NOT

GET ENOUGH SLEEP

# LOOKS

# CAN BE

# DECEIVING

LET YOUR ANGER GO

# STRETCH EVERY MORNING

GROWL WHEN YOU
WANT SOME SPACE

THE SIMPLE THINGS IN
LIFE ARE THE BEST

# STOP

# AND

# LISTEN

LOVE WITHOUT EXPECTATION

ESTABLISH YOUR BOUNDARIES

# GO FOR WALKS EVERY DAY

# STAY CURIOUS

TRY ANYTHING ONCE

STAY CONNECTED

# IT'S NOT JUST ABOUT YOU

# DON'T WORRY WHAT OTHERS THINK OF YOU

PLACE YOUR TRUST WISELY

# TOUGH TIMES NEVER LAST

# ROCK YOUR OWN STYLE

GIVE EVERYBODY ...

... A CHANCE

BE UPFRONT WHEN YOU'RE NOT HAPPY

ACCEPT COMPLIMENTS WELL

# TRY TO

# SHARE

# EVERY DAY

ADAPT TO NEW SURROUNDINGS

# LOVE IS ALL THAT MATTERS

# KEEP A GOOD ...

## ... LIFE BALANCE

BE POSITIVE

FEEL THE FEAR AND DO IT ANYWAY

# DON'T GOSSIP

LIFE IS SIMPLER ...

... WHEN YOU ASK
FOR WHAT YOU WANT

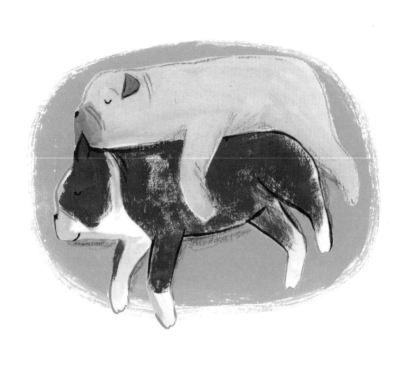

# NO ONE

# IS AN

# ISLAND

LIFE IS TOO SHORT TO BE SAD

DON'T GROW UP

A BEST FRIEND IS FOR LIFE

# EYE CONTACT
# IS EVERYTHING

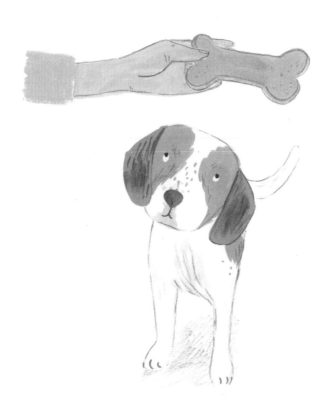

FOLLOW YOUR BLISS

# BEING SMALL DOESN'T MEAN YOU CAN'T DREAM BIG

CARRY YOURSELF WITH CONFIDENCE

# DON'T JUDGE A BOOK BY ITS COVER

# IT'S THE SIZE OF YOUR HEART THAT MATTERS

VARIETY IS THE SPICE OF LIFE

# DON'T TAKE YOURSELF TOO SERIOUSLY

# FRIENDS COME IN ALL SHAPES AND SIZES

ACT FIRST, APOLOGIZE LATER

BE PREPARED

# CHERISH
# LAZY DAYS

EMBRACE ADVENTURE ...

... BUT APPROACH THE
UNKNOWN WITH CAUTION

# DON'T LET THE CRITICS GET YOU DOWN

THERE'S NO SHAME IN
ASKING FOR HELP

# LOVE AT FIRST SIGHT IS REAL

# THE HEART WANTS
# WHAT IT WANTS

PRACTICE ...
MAKES ...
PERFECT!

SEIZE ALL OPPORTUNITIES

KEEP FOCUSED ON YOUR GOAL

# SOMETIMES JUST LISTENING IS BEST

# WE ARE MORE ALIKE THAN DIFFERENT

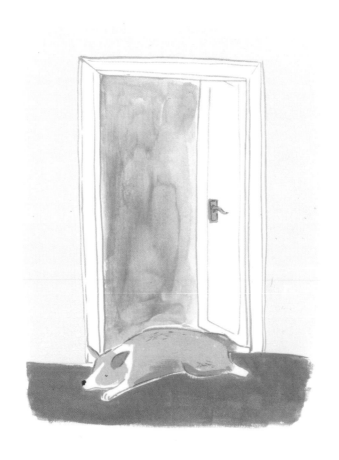

WITH PRACTICE, YOU
CAN NAP ANYWHERE

YOU YOURSELF HOLD THE
KEY TO CONTENTMENT

# BEAUTY IS IN THE
# EYE OF THE BEHOLDER

SOMETIMES

IT'S OKAY TO

BLEND IN

PERSISTENCE PAYS OFF